Lincoln Christian College

WITHDRAWN
University of
Illinois Library
at Urbana-Champaign

NUMBER 701

THE ENGLISH EXPERIENCE

ITS RECORD IN EARLY PRINTED BOOKS
PUBLISHED IN FACSIMILE

THOMAS WHITE

A DISCOVERIE OF BROWNISME... AMONG THE ENGLISH COMPANY OF THE SEPARATION... AT AMSTERDAM

LONDON, 1605

WALTER J. JOHNSON, INC.
THEATRUM ORBIS TERRARUM, LTD.
AMSTERDAM 1974 NORWOOD, N.J.

The publishers acknowledge their gratitude to
the Syndics of Cambridge University Library
for their permission to reproduce the Library's
copy, Classmark: Syn.7.60.160

S.T.C. No. 25408

Collation: $A\text{-}D^4, E^2$

Published in 1974 by

Theatrum Orbis Terrarum, Ltd.
O.Z. Voorburgwal 85, Amsterdam

&

Walter J. Johnson, Inc.
355 Chestnut Street
Norwood, New Jersey
07648

Printed in the Netherlands

ISBN 90 221 0701 9

Library of Congress Catalog Card Number:
74-80226

A DISCOVERIE of Brownisme:

OR,

A briefe declaration of some of the errors and abhominations daily practised and increased among the English company of the seperation remayning *for the present at* Amsterdam *in* Holland.

A wicked man deceiueth his neighbour, and leadeth him into a way that is not good. Pro. 16. 29.

By *Thomas White.*

LONDON
Printed by E. A. for *Nathaniell Fosbroke* and are to be solde at his Shop at the West end of Paules. 1605.

To the Reader.

TWo extremities (dangerous) there are which in thefe dayes bringe no fmall detriment or annoyance to the Church of God. The one Atheiftical prophanes, which is fearful; and the other hipocritical contention, which is abhominable. And thefe howfoeuer they feeme to differ the one from the other, yet the one is ftrengthned and hardned by the other, and this with a mutuall reciprocation:

Againft both thefe, the holy Ghoft applies a foueraigne remedie: *Heb.* 13. 14. *Followe after peace and holines, without which no man cã fee God.* And *Luk*: 1..14.15. *That we being deliuered from our enemies, might ferue him in bolines and righteoufnes* (to auoyde prophanes) *before his face* (to flye hypocrifie) *all our dayes.*

To the Reader.

Of the latter of these, or rather of both, (for the former oft times proceedeth from the latter, howsoeuer for a while enuy palliateth it selfe vnder the name of zeale as both are signified by one Greeke word) I haue giuen an instance in this treatise following in that congregatiō, which God hath made as a spectacle for others to beware of rash, heady, and contentious courses.

ζῆλος

This haue I done (all other peaceable meanes being before vsed) for the discharging of mine owne duety both to God and his Churches, the staying of others, who would neuer be so affected to them as they are, if they knew their fearefull estate.

If eyther for the breuity or rudenes of the stile it satisfie thee not: for the former I cōfesse that I haue rather endeauoured to point at things briefely, then by dilating to fill vp large volumes, of purpose omitting many the vilest thinges, partly for offending chaste eares, partly for sparing them, vnlesse further occasion be ministred by théselues.

And as for the rudenes of the stile, either by

super-

To the Reader.

superfluous repetitions, or redundant speeches, let the inconuenience both of time & place something excuse me, being but newly arriued, neyther enioying health, nor help of bookes in the penning therof; my minde also many waies distracted about other businesses. The time to come may bring foorth some further thing more answerable to thine expectation: In the meane time accept this in the best part. And the Lord giue thee vnderstanding in all thinges.

A BRIEFE DISCOVERYE,
of some of the errors and abhominations, dailye practised and increased, amongst the *English* Companye of the seperation, remaining for the present at *Amsterdam* in Holland.

T may seeme strange, that any, who pretend (aboue all other) sinceritie in Religion, and there-vpon forsake their owne natiue Country, should yet notwithstāding, be found to abound aboue others with all kinde of debate, malice, adulteries, cousonages, and such other like enormities: And that so much the more in the dayes of their banishment and extreame pouertie, which outward affliction, doth euen humble the wicked: And yet so farre from repentance, that when they are shewed and admonished of their euill dealinges, they seeke to couer,

hide,

hide, cloake, reproach and reuile their admonishers of better counsaile; which for mine owne part I could haue borne in silence, committing it to him that iudgeth iustly the sonnes of men: yet least others be deceaued by thē, as some of vs haue beene, and should be drawn by them through their painted colour of holinesse to partake with their abhominations and vnfruitefull workes of darkenes, & to runne with them to that fearefull extreamitie in cōdemning al other churches & men: I thought it my duetie according as my leasure (which is small, & my abilitie which is lesse, would permit) vpō experience to giue warning to others of their leaders euil dealing, wherby their people are deuoured.

And, although I knowe I shall object my selfe heerein but to the reproach of virulent and venemous tongues, yet shall I be content to beare it, that others may reape benefit thereby. Neither doe I this, any way to discourage the true vpright hearted, but rather that all that call vpon the name of the Lord, may learne to cast frō them the cloake of hypocrisie, and the leauen of contention and malicioufnes, and so not in showe, but in deed departe from jniquitie, least they reape the fruites thereof as these haue done.

I haue already written to their leader M. *Fr. Iohnson*, of his (with the rest of their elders) falshood, shiftings, and other contraryties: as also laying to their charge, partaking in and with their church in these blasphemous doctrines.

1. That

A discouery of Brownisme.

1, *That they held it lawfull for a man to liue with her that is not his wife, rather then to reueale himselfe*, which first denyes the prophecy of Christ: secondly destroyes the nature of repentance, and thirdly is a fundamētal error cōtrary to these scriptures. *Math. 3. 2. 8. Rom 3. 8. & 6. 1. Heb. 6.*

2. *That there are qualities in God not essentiall, & that loue in God is not of his being, but that the selfe same loue that is in god, that is also in vs*, which ouerturnes the nature of God, and the simplenes of his being, and is a ground of famulisme, and a blasphemous Doctrine contrary to these scriptures. *Ex. 3. 14. Es. 43, 25. 1. Iohn. 4. 8.*

To this he promised answere and performed it not, though he tooke no small paines by falsifying to discourage the witnesses, but was content to let it lye vpon him vnanswered, so becomming by his own confessiō a dūbe Minister. Now therfore I see no further cause of writing to him, but will turne to the Christian Reader; giuing him a taste of their dealing, both in writing and practise, profession & conuersation, and yet laying that to their charge wherof due proofe can bee made, as the Reader shall well perceiue by my proofes, & their answers iudging indifferently. [Page. 147. Last answ. to M. Iac.]

They indeede are the men, that accuse others of simplicitie, absurdity, inconstancy in turning their coates, of being hearers and not doers of the word, of retayning open offenders & so becomming cages of euery vncleane bird, o: being neither willing [Answere to M. H.]

B   nor

A discouery of Brownisme.

Answer to M. Iun. let:
nor able to iustifie their estate, and this not alone of their country-men but against those Churches also with whome they liue.

1. But what if themselues haue : 1. betrayed their owne cause in writing. 2 Giuen the blacke letter of condenation not alone to the churches of Christ that eyther are, or haue beene since the Apostles daies, but also to theselues, & their practise by their describing of a visible Church?

3. Doe practise that amongst themselues which they condemne vtterly in others, & haue amongst themselues open and notorious cousners, and such other like offendors?

As in the True descrip: of a visible Ch:
4. Haue giuen themselues ouer to Sathan, and brought the curse on their owne heads by wicked and vrgodly excommunications. Are they then *the holy assembly of Saints marching in such a heauenly order after the Lamb, whether soeuer hee goeth, whereunto no vncleane thing entreth, nor remaineth?* whether these accusations bee true or no, let the sequele declare.

And first that Master *Fr. Ih.* hath vtterly disproued the maine drift of all his booke, and so betrayed his owne cause, As Christ alleaged against the

Mat.12.27
Pharises, the example of their owne Children, that they might be their iudges: so may I his owne writings against himselfe, that they may be his iudge, which thus I shew.

Last ans: to *M. Ia.*
The drift of his booke is by the description of a true church, to discouer the false. This discription

as

A discouery of Brownisme.

as oft elsewhere, so also he hath, Page 196. last answer to *M. Iac: viz.*

That a true visible Church of Christ, is a company of faithfull people, called out by the word of God, and seperated from the world, and the false waies thereof, gathered and ioyned together in fellowship of the Gospell, by a voluntary profession of the faith and obedience of Christ. And his meaning of this discription doth further appeare by cōparing it with the third false Doctrine alleadged by him, Page 158. of the same booke, as also with the 17. Art: of ther confession, where hee expoundes it, by seperating his Church from vanitye, Idolatrie, dissolute life, and all false workes of darkenes.

This discription so propounded and expounded, he thus ouerthroweth, page 47. of the same booke before cited, where he affirmeth, *that the Israelites in Egipt were Gods Church,* prooues it by *Exod.* 4. 22. 23. euen then, *while they sinned with the Idols of Egipt,* alleadging *Ezek.* 20. If they committed Idolatrie with the Idols of Egipt, how were they then a company of faithfull people seperated from all false wayes? If he say this their sinne was not their generall estate, as he answers in an other case to M. *H.* Page 49. The place quoted by himselfe out of *Ezek.* 20. shewes the contrary, affirming *none of them to haue forsaken the Idols of Egipt.* If he say this their sin was not of obstinacie, the same scripture sheweth that they were admōished, v. 7. yet they *rebelled against him.* v. 8. And as for the nature of their

Last answ: to. *M. Iac:*

Answ: to M. *H.* page 49.

B 2. jdolatry

jdolatry it was heathenish; will he then say that Idolaters in their generall estate, with heathenish jdolatrie, rebelling atter admonition, are such a faithfull people seperate frõ all falle waies, as he describes a true Church to be? If not, how were they Gods Church?

Cic. orat :
P. Qu.

To vse *Tullies* words, *testimonium tuum quod in aliena re leue est, hoc contra te graue. &c.* Thine owne testimony which in an other case is of small weight, this against thy selfe is of much moment.

And heere he must remẽber that he describeth not a true Church, what it ought to be, but what it is if it bee a true Church as the drift of that place, where this description is set down declares, As that,

Last answ:
to M. Ia:
Page. 196.

1. *It is for the clearing the question betwene them.*
2. *For the discerning of the true church frõ the false.*
3. *Bids M. Iac compare their best asemblies with this description. &c.* Otherwise his aduersary might haue answered, that though the Churches of Englãd agreed not with that descriptiõ, yet might they haue beene true Church's notwithstanding, and he had writtẽ nothing to any purpose against him.

Last answ:
to M. Ia.

Moreouer in the answere to the preface of the same booke, Sect. M *Fr. Ih.* thus speakes: *Any Church though truely constituted, if they will rather abide in error then obey the voice of Christ, are not true churches.* And yet the Iewes in Egipt rebelling after admonition, are Gods church by his account: how well these thinges hang together let the Reader judge. In like mãner *M. Ih.* denies not. page 87.

of

A discouerie of Brownisme.

of the booke before cited, that the Iewes in Chrifts time, yea and after his death, were true Churches, which had defpifed admonition before: *Lu.* 7.30. *Math.* 23. 37. yet this which M. *Iohnf.* acknowledges, M. *H. Barrow* calles blafphemy: fo well they agree together.

Refut. of *Giff.*

Is it pofsible fo to ouerthrow the maine drift of his owne writings, and perceiue it not? Or is it not veryfied which the wife man fpeaketh? *The euill man is fnared by the wickednes of his owne lippes.* And yet this booke he faith he did not make alone, but confulted with others heerein, and namely with Maifter *Ainf-worth*, a man that hath turned his coate as oft as euer *D. B.* if not oftner, whome hee teatmes *approoued in Chrift*: and *Daniel Studly* an elder of ther Church, a man, (not alone for his filthineffe with his wiues Daughter, but alfo for fupporting of manifeft & fhamefull vncleannes and coufning amongft them in others) fitter for the ftewes thē to be an elder in any chriftiā fociety. No better is his dealing in condemning the Dutch & French Churches, for defpifing their admonition, and yet acknowledge the Iewes in Chrift time, to be a true church, difpifing more admonition, and that of greater finnes then euer they admonifhed the Elders ofthefe Churches of: hee that wauereth in his owne teftimony, how fhall his witneffe be receiued? but he is not alone content to confute M. *Ih.viz:* himfelfe, except he doe alfo by his defcription cut off from being true churches in their ac-

Pro. 12. 13
Anfw: to the pref. Sect. 1.

As namely in *Iudith Holder* and others.

ἀπὸ τῆς αὐτῆς ἔχει ἴσην.

B 3   count

count, all the churches of Christ that euer haue bin since the Apostles daies: 2. now are, yea and 3 theselues which thus I prooue.

If no church that hath beene since the Apostles daies or now is that we reade of, be seperate from al false waies in their accompt, then by his description and in their account must they be no true churches, but the former is true: therefore the latter.

The proposition is vndeniable from his owne description.

The Assumption is as certaine, as will appeare, in that they account the very vsing of the Lords Prayer as a Prayer, to be a false way, which was vsed from the Apostles age, as *Tertullian* saith: *Premissa legitima & ordinaria oratione, ius est superstruendi extrinsecus petitiones. &c.* The lawfull and ordinary prayer (speaking of the Lordes prayer) being premised, &c.

Tertul: lib. de orat:

2. For the Churches that now are, their dealing with the Dutch and French Churches declare it sufficiently: & howsoeuer they seeme to put difference betweene those churches in the Low Countries whome they haue admonished, and those that they haue not; yet to put the matter out of doubt, let him tell vs if they account it not Apostacy for one of them, so much as once to heare the word preached in any congregation Dutch or French in all the Lowe Countries besides. Or if he can, let him name any one church on the face of the earth now, that holdeth not false wayes, yea euen in their

constitu-

A diſcouery of Browniſme.

conſtitution in their account: Neyther ſhall he ſhift off the matter with his diſtinction of faultye and falſe worſhippe, for when hee hath put downe the difference, whereby he diſtinguiſheth the one from the other, which yet he hath not done to my remēbrance, then wil I ſhew him that there is no church that he can mentiō beſides themſelues, that holdes not onely faulty, but falſe waies alſo in their account, and that in their conſtitution.

Are not they then the blaſphemers of the Chriſtians and their churches? Or is not this to robbe Chriſt of his honour? Or may not that ſaying. *Pro.* 11. 12. bee veryfied of themſelues: *Baz leregnehu chaſar leb. He that deſpiſeth his neighbour is a foole.*

3. But heerein others may pardon them, for they are as fauourable to others as to themſelues, for except themſelues be agreeable to their owne deſcription, after wounding others, they haue turned the point of their weapon into their owne bowels: that they are not ſeperate from all open offenders, and all falſe wayes appeares.

1. In that they retaine amongſt them open offendors: to giue inſtance, one *Caſtle* was noted amongſt themſelues publikely in their meeting for couſnage, and that by one of their elders, and indeede knowne notoriouſly ſo to bee, which if M. *Ih.* doubts of, he may aske his elder *Sta: Mercer,* their Deacon: *Tho. Biſhop: W. Knowling, Robert Ickſon* &c. And yet would M. *Ih.* with his teacher M. *A.* and the reſt of their elders, defend that hee

ought

ought not to bee publiquely dealt withall for it, because it was not orderly made publique: and this before many witnesses: neyther did that *Castle* shew any repentance in like sorte of this sinne.

Mr. P. I. L. W. N. and others.

Robert Bayly.

Besides him was not *R B.* (after other moste horrible adultery) publikelye accused in their meeting for creeping in at a windowe to come to bed to another mans wife in her husbands absence, yet was this man neuer publiquely dealt withall, vntill this day for it, that I can learne. Or if these instances serue not their turne, what will they say to their Elder, *Daniel Studley*? (who together with his filthines afore mentioned, in supporting vncleanes in a woman a member of their church) did also refuse to pray with his owne wife a member likewise of the same Church, and yet will shew no repentance for thus doing, though he hath beene dealt withall for it; yea and worse carryage then this, of which his wife hath often and doth continually complaine, which though he be not ashamed to commit, yet I am ashamed to mencyon. I am sure M. *Ih* cannot pretend ignorance heerein, for hee hath beene tolde oft of his euill dealing though hee durst not, or would not redresse it. Or if these yet bee not enough, you shall haue more (if neede be) as *Iudith Holder, Canady, Iaacob Iohnson &c.* How are they thē seperate from all open offenders? or are they not defiled by cōmunicating with such? Or shall I say fitte members for such a fellowshippe? If they say this is not in their constitutiō, I answere yes euen in their

H. C.

A discouery of Brownisme.

the constitution they holde false waies, which thus I prooue.

1. In their constitution they holde. First that the Lords prayer is not to be vsed as a Prayer, contrary to chrifts expresse comaundment, which is neyther against reason nor proportion of faith. Secodly, contrary to the tenor of the words, hauing the forme of a prayer in all things, as *Our Father, giue vs*, and *amen* annexed in the end, which shewes that they are petitions not positions or rules which are set downe in another forme. *Mat.* 77. et 21.22. 1. *Ioh.* 5 14. Thirdly, contrary to the vse of al christians, that wee reade of, as before out of *Tertullian* and others may be alleadged:

2. They hold also that it is not lawfull for the innocent partyes, to retaine the offeder, as the wife her husbad, or the husband his wife, if either party haue committed adultery, no though the innocet party vpon the others repentance, forgiuing the others sinne, be desirous still to liue with the other party in the marriage couenant as before, but haue excomunicated the parties innocent for so doing, as namely *H.C.* & one *Homes his* wife, vpon this, diuers of them accused themselues of adulterye, that so they might be ridde of their wiues, as namely one *W. Holder* and *Tho: Canady.*

3. They haue altered many thinges which they held in their constitution, as among other, that *it was not lawful for Apostates to beare office*, then must they confesse that they did hold false waies in their constitu-

A discouery of Brownisme.

constitution, and so by consequent, then were no true Churches.

4. But what would it profit them to be free from false waies in their constitution, if their practise bee not according to their profession?

Answ: to M.H: This (to vse their owne wordes) makes their sin the more greeuous. And sith their knowledge is but in part aswell as their loue, are not they as well as others subiect to erre in constitution as well as practise? If M. *Fr: Iohnson* with his other helpers should yet finde out a further shift, & say that their meaning in their description afore mentioned, is, that *A true church must be seperate frō all false waies, which they see,* for the preuenting of them therein, I answere:

1. If they had ment onely such false waies, it had beene needefull in the description to haue implyed so mnch.

2. Though they haue beene already pressed with exceptions against this discription, yet haue they no where as yet taken vp this starting hole that I can perceiue.

3. Yet if now they should, they haue stopped it thēselues, Page. 107. 108. 127. of *his last answere to M. Iac.* and in other places of their writings.

4. Let them minde, whether enough hath not beene shewed them for the clearing of these errors in their constitution before cited.

5. Whether they giue not their aduersaries aduantage if they should thus answere:

Besides

A Discouery of Brownisme.

Besides that there bee false waies, which though they were held of ignorance, would disanul a company so gathered, from being Gods Church notwithstanding.

Thus haue they paued their way with snares, to entrappe themselues. Had not the simple neede to take heede how they take vp wares vpon their credit? And haue they not abused the world that publish in print, *that they neyther receiue nor retaine any such as care not how they borrow and make no conscience to pay againe?* I doubt not but their owne hearts know how false this is, in *Io. Nicholas* and others. — Page. 202, last answ: to *Ia*.

And heere it shall not be amisse to put downe a briefe opposition betweene their *true description of a visible Church, and their practise*: that so the Reader may the better perceiue the difference between their profesison & practise, & this onelye in some few knowne particulars, by this description. First for the Pastor: — Treatise so entituled.

1. The Pastor must bee indued with much patience: but their Pastor with much impaciencye, as hath appeared not alone in his dealing with *M. Ad:* and his Brother *G:I.* and his threatning to forsake his owne congregation when he was crossed of his minde: all which are discouered alreadye by his brother: Page 126. 143. 144. and knowne to be true by other witnesses, but also in other particulars whereof some shall be after mencioned. *An angry man stirreth vp strife and a furious man abounndeth* — Of his booke entituled *A discourse of certaine troubles and excom. &c.*

C 2

A discouery of Brownisme.

deth in transgression.

2. The Pastor of the true Church must be louing & cōpassionate, but their Pastor vnnatural & vnmerciful, & that to his own father, yea for the time which his Father was with his Brother *G. I.* hee would not so much as once see him, or relieue his necessitie, though he were not yet excommunicated frō thē This I heard iustified to his face before many witnesses, and he could not deny it: *so true it is, that he that begetteth a foole, begetteth himselfe sorrow,* as the wise man speaketh. For the teacher:

By M.S.
Pro.17.21.
& 20.20.

1. The teacher of a true Church is sincere: their teacher steined with Hypocrisie, as in his dealing concerning *G.I,M.Sl:*

2. The teacher of a true Church must bee vnreprooueable: but their teacher is spotted againe and againe with Apostasie in their account as before hath beene noted.

1.Tim,3.

3, The teacher of the true Church must take diligent care to keepe the Church from errors: their teacher hath beene a meanes to bring in, and defend false Doctrines, as the latter of those two before mencioned and others that may bee alleaged. For the Elders:

1. The Elders of a true Church must bee indued with the spirit of God: their Elder *Da: St:* with the spirit of vncleanes.

2. The Elders of a true church must see the lawes of God kept: their Elder would defend the transgresing of them in himselfe and others.

3. The

A discouery of Brownisme.

3. The Elders of a true church doe gouerne their owne houses orderly: but the Elder mencioned most disorderly as elsewhere is cited.

4. The Elders aforesaid must bee louing: their Elder *D:St:* cruell and tyranicall, in so much that some of their owne mēbers haue complained, that if they had a matter as cleare as the sunne against him, yet durst they not deale with him for it. Before M. *Powell* and others.

5. The elders of a true church, must be vnreproueable: but their Elder *St: Mer:* hath (as their teacher) beene noted for Apostasie. For the Deacons:

1. The Deacons of the true Church of Christ, must haue a pure conscience & must not bee giuen to filthy lucre. But their Deacon *Christoph: Bow:* for his deceiuing of many poore, euē of their owne companye, of halfe that which the Magistrates of *Narden* had giuen them weekelye, was thereupon (when it came to light) through widdow *Colgates* meanes called *Iudas* the purse-bearer in *Narden* for so doing: Not to speake of many such like instances that by him may be giuen. And for the Elders ioyntly:

1. The church of Christ doe priuately admonish a priuate sin of a holy & louing affection: but their Elders could call, *R:W:* before thē in the first place, for a priuate thing: & threatē her excōmunication for that which after ward for shame they let fall.

And for the peoples vncleanes, cousning, disgracing, backe-biting, & vndermining one of another amongst themselues, it is a thing so common and well wellknowne of them at home and abroad, that I neede not in this place to speake further of it, heauen and earth can beare me witnesse against thē in those things: oh that they would apply vnto themselues and their practise that which the Prophet *Ieremie* speakes! *Will they steale, murther and commit adulterie &c. And yet crie the temple of the Lord, the temple of the Lord?*

Are these then this beautifull? yea moste wonderful church, rauishing the sences to conceiue of it? are these the Saints then marching in such a heauenly and gracious aray, where euery stone hath his beauty, his burthen, and his order, where no law is wrongfully wrested, or wilfully neglected, no truth hid or peruerted? or rather haue they not deluded many poore soules, with such sweete wordes, who when they haue seene their estate, and their expectations so frustrated haue vsed these wordes: They neede neuer seperate themselues, if they liue thus: for any Godly societie wil quickely thrust them out from them so practising as they doe.

W.F, & E.H.

Certainely this their *description of a visible Church* is as cleare a testimony, and as pregnant a sentence of condemnation against themselues and their practise as may be possible.

But yet that their hypocrisie may further appeare, let me giue the reader a taste also of their dealing in condemning others, euen in those things that they would and doe practise themselues, & that in these particulers.

1. They

1. They condemne others, for communicating with open offenders and yet practise it themselues as is before shewed. *Page. 157.*

2. For making men to sweare to accuse themselues, yet *M. Ih.* practised the same to one *I.L*, and it is moreouer a common practise among them, both publikely and priuately, so to doe, yet would their Elder *Dan. Studly* neuer so much as denye the matter of incest with his wiues Daughter, for the clearing of himselfe, though hee were requested for the satisfying of weake Btetheren so to doe. *Page. 63 Iohn Laxden.*

3. They condemne the Dutch churches, for baptising the seede of those that are not members of their church, and yet *M. Iohnson* with the rest could offer to receiue *M. Deuksberies* childe to Baptisme, and were offended at *G: I:* for witstanding it: and yet he neyther was, nor would ioyne himselfe as a member vnto them. *Answ: to Inn. letters page George Ioh.*

4. In like manner doe they deale with the Dutch churches of *Amsterdam,* for hauing but one church in the Cittie. And yet *M. Iohnson* to vrge others to ioyne to them: (which for diuers disorders amongst them would not so doe) could alleadge that there was no warrant for two seuerall churches to be in one city in the scriptures. *Consisting of so greate a multitude*

5. In the place aboue quoted, they giue the like sentence against the Dutch and French Churches, for deciding matters by the elders, without the body of the church, and not suffring in this respect

the

the 18. of *Mat* rightly to be obserued amōgst them: and yet their Elders, viz: *M. Fr: Ih. and his fellowes*, could decide one *T. Canadyes* matter, who had ac-

Of adulte-ry.

cused himselfe to be rid of his wife, and this without their knowledge or consent: But the said *Canady* not resting in the Elders determination, brought it to their Church, alleadging that he had

W. Holder.

iniury done to him, in that *W. H* could bee seperate frō his wife on his owne accusation of himselfe of adultery, & he could not. And further to iustify the bringing of matters in the third place to their Elders (for so they practise before the matter bee brought to the whole church) they could alleadge the very same reasons against *M. P.* that they had before condemned in the Dutch. And for the 18, *of Mat.* how it is made a matter of partialitie and enuie, yea a cloake to couer filthines withal at eueuery pinch amōgst them, would grieue ones heart to consider.

6. They condemne the Dutch & French aforesaid for worshipping God in the Idoll Temples of Antichrist, yet themselues suffer their poore to receiue the almes of the Dutch, which is a Sacrifice, *Phil.* 4. 18. in the same place: and if they giue thāks in receiuing their almes (as duety both to God & man bindes them to doe) Then doe they likewise worship God in the Idoll Temples: neyther will it helpe them to say that it is not publique worship, which if they could prooue, yet the commaūdement *Deut.* 12. if it be moral, as they account it,

and

A discouery of Brownisme.

and must bee executed on these temples, then no ciuill vse of them may be had at all; much lesse spirituall.

7. They witnesse against the Dutch, for vsing the censure of suspension: And yet themselues, could suspend M. *S.* many moneths together before his excommunication, a man for learning & giftes worthy of his preferment among the dutch, and to good too be of their fellowship.

They condemne in others nonresidency, And yet their Deacon *D. Br.* could neere three quarters of a yere be absent frō their church, saue that twise or thrice, about his Maisters businesse, hee came ouer from *London* to *Amsterdam* to buye and sell wares. And this without any leaue of their church at *Amsterdam* so to doe. How did hee that hath an Office waite on his Office? Page. 65. Last answ: to *H.I.*

Rom. 12.

9. Lastly, they passe the like sentence on the Dutch, for becomming one body, with excommunicates, when as they excommunicate their owne members onely for hearing the word so much as preached amongst the Dutch or French, yet are they one body with an excommunicate from the French church themselues. I might heere also note their like dealing with the Dutch, for their obseruation of certaine Holy daies: yet doe these mē obserue these holy daies as much as the Dutch, as well in shutting their shops, as also hauing their publique meetings for worshippe on these daies: Neyther haue they in so many yeares M. *Ih.* &c.

M. *Fr: Ih:* and the rest.

D   space

A discouery of Brownisme.

space had time to debate and discusse this matter among them, as M. *Ioh. Answered, Sect.* 3. *to the Preface,* fiue yeares agoe. But it would be long and teadious to bring the manifolde examples that in this kinde may be alleadged, but vntill further an-answere, these may suffice. Now let me aske them, Are these things euill in others and good in them? or as the Poet speakes: *iustũ non iustum non iustum-iustum quod vobis libet:* or wil they say as *Medea in* Ouid, *video meliora probóq̃ deteriora sequor?* But rather wil they heare the Apostle *Rom.*2.1.3. What art thou that condemnest another and doest the same? Or the prophet *Ps.*50.16, Why takest thou my word in thy mouth & hatest to be reformed? Or Christ himselfe, hypocrite first cast the beame out of thine owne &c *Mat.*7.5. One would little thinke that knew not their euill dealing that euer they would snatch vp that to serue their owne turne, which they condemne in others.

And heere although I might declare their false and impertinent allegation of Scripture, as if it were no sinne to take the name of God in vaine & make the Scripture serue their fancy; but because this hath beene done already in part by *G, I.* in his booke page 85, which yet lyeth on them vnanswered, and vpon further occasion may be further manifested: I will passe by this, as also their false accusations of whole Chuches, as will appeare by comparing the 7.² accusatiõ, with the practice of the Duch Churches, and come to the 4. thing

Of the last answ: to M Ia:

Plautus.

ᶜ Neh.6.8. Pro.24.28. Confess: with *Iun:* let:page.54

that

A Discouery of Brownisme.

that I proposed, namely, to shewe how they haue drawne the curſſe of God on themſelues by raſh, vniuſt and wicked excommunication.

1 And heere I may ſpeak of 27 or there abouts euen one halfe of them, at that time, and that of the elder ſorte: which all within a very ſhort ſpace were caſt out for refuſing to come being ſent for, to the meeting of the other part, although they anſwered, that on the ſuddaine they could not come at ſo ſhort ſpace and warning, for diuers buſines, but would come at any other time which on both ſides ſhould bee thought conuenient, And although one of thē *H. A.* was diſtracted in minde: but they ſpared none, & this excommunication was confirmed by the Paſtor *M. Ih.* Howbeit, afterward was this excommunication repealed with faſting and prayer, and acknowledged to be raſh and vniuſt, and all receiued in againe, and they that withſtood their receauing in, were on the other ſide excommunicated. Notwithſtanding, after this againe, becauſe their Paſtor was vrged to acknowledge his ſinne by one of thē *C. S.* they were all turned out againe. Such dallying with the Lords ordnances is fearefull. *W. A.*

2. As alſo how they deliuered diuers to Sathan for hearing the word preached in the Dutch church, though ſome were encouraged by their paſtor and teacher ſo to doe, and promiſed to bee borne out in it by themſelues, as namely M *S.* yet after they brake, promiſe with him & caſt him out.

3. Or what will they say to this? M. *Iohnson* with diuers others of their leaders, put downe reasons vnder their hands, that Apostates might not beare office from the Scriptures, and so practised: yet after that M. *Ainsworthes* Apostasie was discouered, to keepe him in office, they altered their judgement and practise, and *W. A.* those that would not be brought to their will, they cast out likewise; although they would neuer answere their owne reasons in writing, in like sorte as they had set them downe: no nor suffer their owne reasons to be read in their meeting, being requested therunto. Is not this to play Sathās part to bring men to distruction, and not vse as good meanes to recouer them out againe? M. *Ad.* for lesse Apostasie was not suffered to beare an inferior office among them.

Williā Asplen. Besides, they haue cast out *W. A*, for recalling a former Schisme: yet the said *W. A.* did & still doth stand to that acknowledgement which was vnder his hand, wherewith all they were satisfied. Of this I with others haue written to them, but could get no answere; yet that schisme was for not appealing to the Dutch Churches: and if they doe appeale, then hath *M. Ih.* with the rest refused vtterly to be tryed by them.

Before his departing from them,

5. Others they haue likewise accursed, that being the parties innocēt desired to liue with the parties offendors, as man and wife together, as before they did in the marriage couenāt, vpon forgiuenes
of

A discouerie of Brownisme.

of their sin of adultery as already is mencioned in *H C.* & one *Homes* his wife. *Hen. Cooke.*

Another woman they excommunicated, because shee brought not her Childe to Baptisme to them, when her husbãd had forbid her in any case so to doe, who had likewise reprooued diuers grosse abuses amongst thẽ, and could receiue neyther answere nor due repentance thereof frõ them; the woman alleaged that *Tymothies* mother was a faithfull woman, and one that brought vp her son in the feare of God from his Child-hood, yet did she not circumcise him: and no other cause mencioned, but that his Father was a *Grecian.* 1. *Tim.* 4. 6. 2. *Tim.* 1.5. *Act.*16,3. whereunto shee could get no answere. Their [a] Doctor indeede said, that *Tymothies* mother was dead, and so he might haue said of *Moses*, and the Prophets too.

[a] And the onely Doctor in the world in their account.

Their Pastor Maister *F.I.* made doubt of that Scripture, and staid her excommunication, as saying he would not consent to it: yet after the womã had a little vnfoulded his euill dealing, the same Maister *F.Ih.* at the same time, could change his note and say, if that none else would, yet would he be the man that should excommunicate her. And indeede afterward they so did, and all that would not yeild to her excõmunicatiõ, as namely Mistris *S.* Widdowe Ch : and *R. R.* though the chiefe [b] magistrate of the cittie forbid them so to doe. Diuers other reasons were alleadged about this matter, which we shal haue time to relate, after that we

[b] The head haue skout.

haue seene their answere to this, if they will be at leasure so to doe. Now may I not wish that they had not verified the Orators saying? *He that once passeth the boundes of modesty, becommeth impudent out of measure.*

Thus doe they abuse the holy ordinance of God to satisfie their owne reuenging stomacks, *non ita precipitanter in quenquam torquendum.* Is this the long suffering spirit of meekenes in recouering and seeking the lost?

Pol.virg: li: 4°.cap.12

Or doe they not knowe that the curse is not in vaine, if it cleaues not to them to whome it is giuen it lights on the giuer? Are not then their Bulls of excommunications so many curses on their owne pates? shall I say to vse their owne allegation out of the Prophet, *As he loued cursing so shall it come vnto him, and as he loued not blessing, so shall it be farre from him, and as hee cloathed himselfe with cursing like a rayment, so shall it come into his bowells like water, and like oyle into his bones?* Surelye God that will not holde him guiltles that taketh his name in vaine, will neuer such profanation of his name and ordinance to goe in vaine.

Ps.109.17. 18.

Ex.20.7.

And for some of them that are by these accursed I know they haue learned Christ otherwise then so, as to feare the cursse causeles. The Lord promised to *Abraham* whose children they are, euen manye which they haue cast out, that hee would *blesse them that blesse thee, and curse them that cursse thee.&c.* And let them say as *Dauid* of *Shimei*, It may

Gen. 12.3.
2.Sam. 16. 12.

A discouery of Brownisme.

may bee the Lord will doe vs good for their curſing this day, yea, let them acknowledge Gods goodneſſe towards them in drawing them out of their Tents, as I dœ his mercy towards me in keeping me frō ioyning with thē, being yet ſometimes addicted too much vnto thē, before I perceiued their fearefull eſtate. I could cite many other things yet viler, as their Sauadge and cruell dealing to fatherleſſe Children: as namely Maiſter *P.* and Maiſter *B.* his Children, and other ſuch like.

But I like not now to ſaile further in this Ocean, but will content my ſelfe with the confeſsion of their owne members, *W.C.* I thought (ſaid he) *that they had beene all Saints, but I haue found them all deuils;* and this before many witneſſes: yet is this man ſtill a member amongſt them. And for theſe excommunicators the Lord giue them grace to repent, that they may neuer haue their portion among the curſed, to heare that fearefull ſentence, Goe ye curſed: which is the thing I wiſh them from my heart. Amen.

W. Clerk.

Since then they haue confuted their owne writings, and giuen the black ſentence of condemnation to the other Churches of Chriſt that haue beene, yea and themſelues, by their deſcription, and practiſe that amongſt themſelues which they condemne in others: let others take heede howe they pertake in thier ſinnes, leaſt alſo they taſte of their fond excommunications.

And for the prophane (not to ſpeake here of the popiſh

popish factiō drowned in superstitiō, whose fruites are treachery) let them not heerby be hardned the more in thier sinne, & prophanes, but rather seeing they that striue if they striue not lawfully, doe yet misse of the marke they ayme at; what shall bee the end of those that set not forward at all in the waies of God? let them remember that the gate is
Math.7.13 straite and the way narrow that leadeth to life, & the fewnes of those that finde it. And for the Israel of God, The Lord giue them holynesse &
Heb.12.14 peace, without the which, they shall neuer see him to their comfort.

Hee that causeth the righteous to goe astray by an euill way, shall fall into his owne pit. Pro. 28.10.

Thine in Christ.
Tho: White.

Since I had finished this treatise, I heare that *Tho: Canady* before mencioned, hath liued in *Sodometry* with his Boy, as the Apostle speakes of the hea-
Rom.1. then, *men with men wrought filthines, &c.* and notwithstanding his great wayling, is now cast out, wherin it seemeth they haue forgotten their won-
Mat.18.22 ted allegation: *If thy brother sinne against thee not alone vntil seauen times, but seuenty times seauen, thou shalt forgiue him: If hee returne againe and say it re-*
Luc.17.4. *penteth me.&c.*

Certaine

Certaine briefe reasons proouing the vse of the Lords prayer as a Prayer.

1. AN expresse commaundement neyther contrary to nature, nor analogy of Faith, and agreeable also to the drift and tenor of the place, ought litterally to bee vnderstood and obeyed.

But this, Mat. *6. 9.* ὅταν ἂν &c. And *Luc.* 11. 2. λέγετε πατὴρ ἡμῶν say our Father, &c. is such an expresse commaundement &c. ergo It is also so to be vnderstood and vsed.

2. If Christ had taught onely to pray to this effect, then had he taught nothing but that which *Iohns* Disciples and al the faithful practised before: for the Prayers of the Saints, as of *Salomon, Nehemiah, Daniel,* were to that effect before.

3. Whatsoeuer Scripture hath in euery respect the forme of Prayer, that is not alone matter of Doctrine, but hath beene vsed also as Prayer.

But this Scripture Math. *6. 9.* hath in euery respect

A discoueric of Brownisme.

spect the forme of Prayer. as, *Our Father*, *giue vs*, *leade vs*, and *amen*, *annexed in the end: ergo*. And indeed how can they tell, which were Prayers and which not, if not by their forme of Petition? wherby they are distinguished from Doctrines, & rules proposed in an other forme, as Mat.7.7.& 21.22, 1.Ioh.5,14.

4. In a duety to bee vsed of all, the holy Ghost is plaine: but if those very words are not to bee vsed as a Prayer, no christian for 1500. yeares & more, did vnderstand our Lords meaning.

But they say that the Apostles neuer vsed those very wordes in prayer I answere:

1. An expresse commaundemēt is warrant sufficient without example.

2. There is no example in the whole booke of Gen: of the obseruation of the Sabaoth for 2369. yeares space after the institution of it. Gen.2. Neither to come nearer, is their any example of Baptising, *in the name of the Father*, *Sonne and holy Ghost*) yet is the commaundement of Christ sufficient warrant so to doe. Compare Math.28.19. with Act. 10.28. &.19.5.

3. It is the *Anabaptists* reasoning against childrens baptisme, asking for an example, whē otherwise there is sufficient warrant so to doe, yet are their Pretences as good or better then *M: Iohnsons* in refusing obedience to our Lords commaundement for want of an example.

4. The Prayers mencioned in the new Testament,

A discouery of Brownisme.

ment, are such as were poured foorth vpon speciall occasion as Act. 4. 24. Ioh. 17.

5. Let them shewe mee an example where euer the Apostles prayed before their Sermons; if they can.

F I N I S.

Errata.

IN the Preface the first line, leaue out (dangerous) for Luc. 1. 14. 15. reade Luc. 1. 74. 75. For *H. C.* read *H Cooke*. Page. 10. in the margent For latter, (reade former.) Page 14, line 22.

Date Due

Lincoln Christian College